for Itzhak Perlman

T0210272

Three Pieces from
SCHINDLER'S LIST

From the Universal Motion Picture SCHINDLER'S LIST

Violin and Piano

JOHN WILLIAMS

Theme from
"SCHINDLER'S LIST"

JEWISH TOWN
(Krakow Ghetto – Winter '41)

REMEMBRANCES

ISBN 978-0-7935-3584-2

Visit Hal Leonard Online at
www.halleonard.com

HAL•LEONARD®
CORPORATION

7777 W. BLUEMOUND RD. P.O. BOX 13819 MILWAUKEE, WI 53213

During the summer of 1993 it was my great privilege to compose music for Steven Spielberg's brilliant film *Schindler's List*.

The film's ennobling story, set in the midst of the great tragedy of the Holocaust, offered an opportunity to create not only dramatic music, but also themes that reflected the more tender and nostalgic aspects of Jewish life during these turbulent years.

For this part of the soundtrack I featured a solo violin, accompanied by the Boston Symphony Orchestra, and our greatest good fortune was to have Itzhak Perlman as soloist for the recording.

Included here are three pieces – "Theme from Schindler's List", "Jewish Town (Krakow Ghetto – Winter '41)", and "Remembrances" – which embody the main thematic elements of the score, and it is especially gratifying to me that this music can now be available for performance independent of the film.

John Williams

For Itzhak Perlman
Theme From "SCHINDLER'S LIST"

John Williams

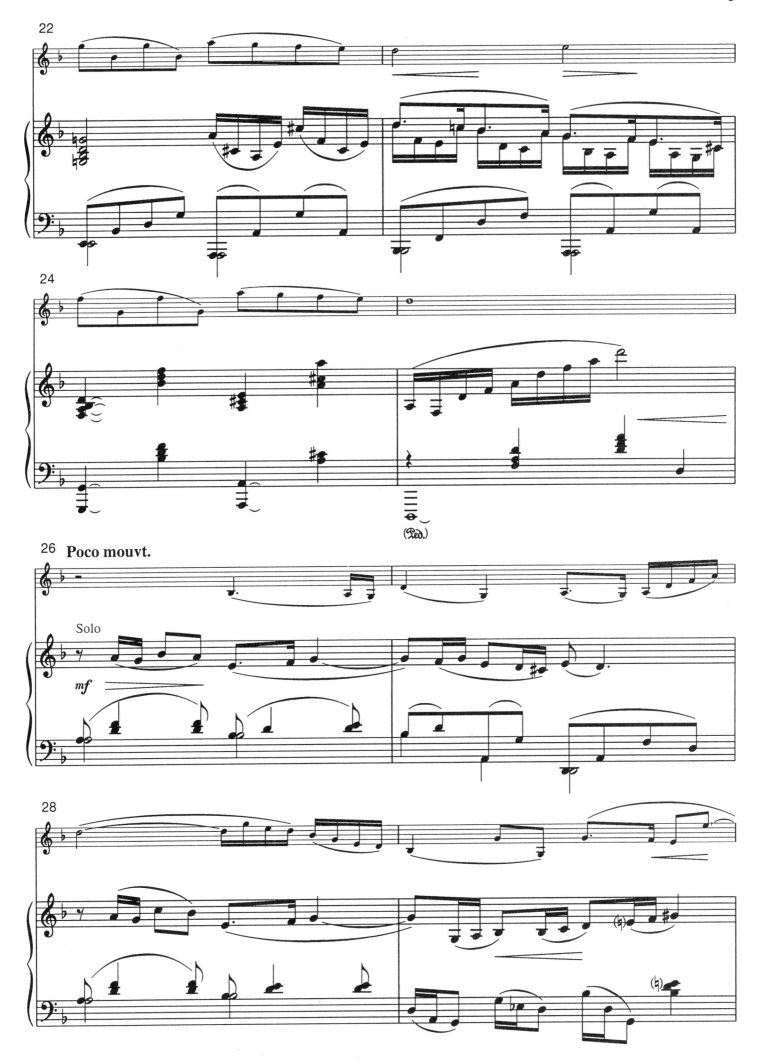

For Itzhak Perlman

Jewish Town
(Krakow Ghetto — Winter '41)

John Williams

Violin

for Itzhak Perlman

Three Pieces from
SCHINDLER'S LIST

From the Universal Motion Picture SCHINDLER'S LIST

Violin and Piano

JOHN WILLIAMS

Theme from
"SCHINDLER'S LIST"

JEWISH TOWN
(Krakow Ghetto – Winter '41)

REMEMBRANCES

ISBN 978-0-7935-3584-2

Visit Hal Leonard Online at
www.halleonard.com

HAL•LEONARD®
CORPORATION
7777 W. BLUEMOUND RD. P.O. BOX 13819 MILWAUKEE, WI 53213

For Itzhak Perlman

Theme From "SCHINDLER'S LIST"

Violin

John Williams

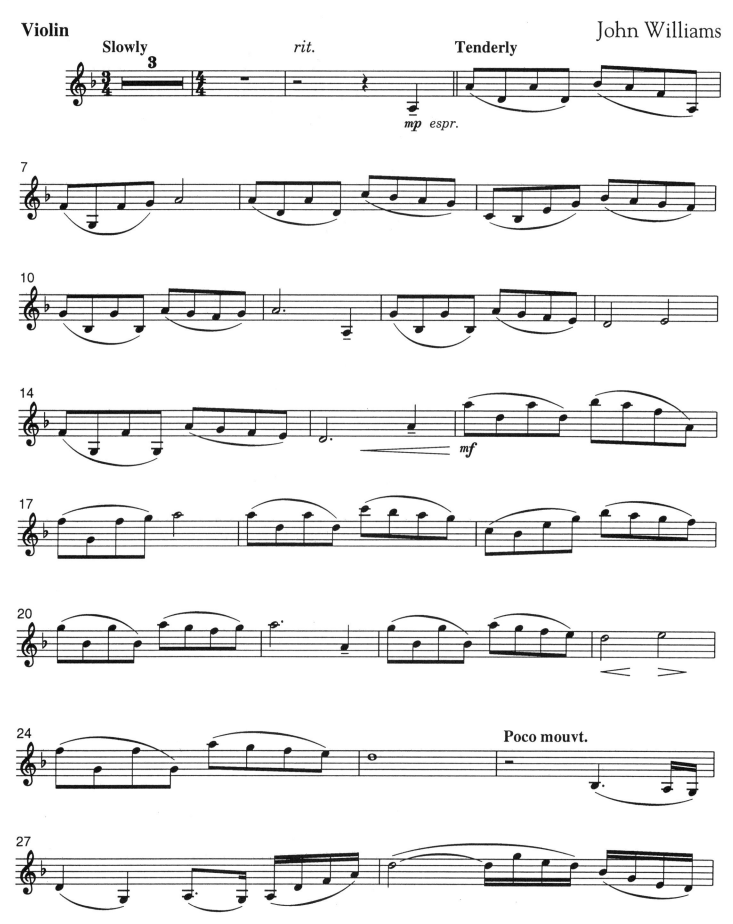

Violin

For Itzhak Perlman
Jewish Town
(Krakow Ghetto — Winter '41)

Violin

John Williams

For Itzhak Perlman
Remembrances

Violin

John Williams

For Itzhak Perlman
Remembrances

John Williams